D0754447

INVISIBLE WORLDS

Atoms and Molecules

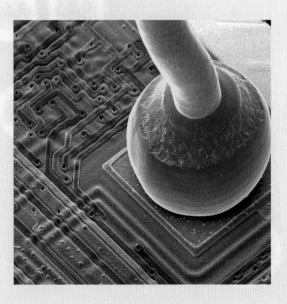

Nathan Lepora

Marshall Cavendish
Benchmark
New York

Published by Marshall Cavendish Benchmark
An imprint of Marshall Cavendish Corporation

Website: www.marshallcavendish.us

This publication represents the opinions and views of the author based on Nathan Lepora's personal experience, knowledge, and research. The information in this book serves as a general guide only. The author and publisher have used their best efforts in preparing this book and disclaim liability rising directly and indirectly from the use and application of this book.

Other Marshall Cavendish Offices:
Marshall Cavendish International (Asia) Private Limited, 1 New Industrial Road, Singapore 536196 • Marshall Cavendish International (Thailand) Co Ltd. 253 Asoke, 12th Flr, Sukhumvit 21 Road, Klongtoey Nua, Wattana, Bangkok 10110, Thailand • Marshall Cavendish (Malaysia) Sdn Bhd, Times Subang, Lot 46, Subang Hi-Tech Industrial Park, Batu Tiga, 40000 Shah Alam, Selangor Darul Ehsan, Malaysia

Marshall Cavendish is a trademark of Times Publishing Limited

All websites were available and accurate when this book was sent to press.

Library of Congress Cataloging-in-Publication Data
Lepora, Nathan.
Atoms and molecules / by Nathan Lepora.
p. cm. — (Invisible worlds)
"Describes the fascinating details and characteristics of atoms and molecules that are too small for the unaided eye to see"—Provided by publisher.
Includes bibliographical references and index.
ISBN 978-0-7614-4192-2
1. Atoms—Juvenile literature. 2. Molecules—Juvenile literature.
3. Integrated circuits—Juvenile literature. 4. Nanotechnology—Juvenile literature. I. Title.
QC173.16.L47 2010
539.7—dc22   2008037237

Series created by The Brown Reference Group
www.brownreference.com

For The Brown Reference Group:
Editor: Leon Gray
Designer: Joan Curtis
Picture Managers: Sophie Mortimer and Clare Newman
Picture Researcher: Sean Hannaway
Illustrator: MW Digital Graphics
Managing Editor: Miranda Smith
Design Manager: David Poole
Editorial Director: Lindsey Lowe
Children's Publisher: Anne O'Daly

Consultant: Dr. Donald R. Franceschetti

Front cover: Science Photo Library/CERN; inset: Shutterstock/Marcin-linfernum

The photographs in this book are used by permission and through the courtesy of:
Corbis: EPA 41; Science Photo Library: 31 (inset), A. Barrington Brown 31 (top), CERN 13, 24, Colin Cuthbert 9, Christian Darkin 43, Delf University of Technology 39, Kenneth Eward/Biografix 30, Dr Tim Evans 27, Eye of Science 7, 45, Mark Garlick 21, Dr Peter Harris 42, Tom Kinsbergen 17, Andrew Lambert Photography 15, Lawrence Berkeley Laboratory 14, McGill University, Rutherford Museum/Emilio sere Visual Archives/American Institute of Physics 16, Dr Gopal Murti 29, Northwestern University 36, David Parker 44, Pasieka 4–5, 34, Philippe Psalia 37, Antoine Rosset 23, Volker Steger 40, Andrew Syred 1, 8, 33, 35, U.S. Department of Energy 19, 20, 22, Mark J. Winter 28, Charles D. Winters 10; Shutterstock: Aga & Miko Arsat 11, Ivan Josifovic 25.

Printed in Malaysia (T)
1 3 5 6 4 2

Contents

Introducing Atoms and Molecules

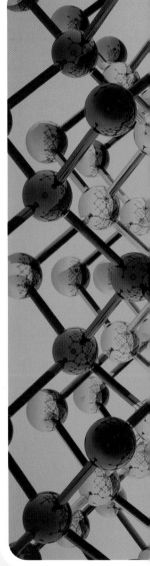

Everything in the world is made up of atoms. These tiny particles join together to form **molecules**. Some molecules are tiny. For example, one molecule of water has only two hydrogen atoms joined to one oxygen atom. However, other molecules grow into giant structures built from billions of atoms. Living things, such as the human body, are made from networks of molecules.

Understanding the seemingly invisible world of atoms is very important. The electronic parts of modern computers are just a few hundred atoms across. In the future, scientists will be able to build computers and other machines from an even smaller number of atoms. This so-called nanotechnology will change people's lives in new and exciting ways.

A diamond is a giant network of carbon atoms. Billions of carbon atoms link together to form the diamond molecule.

CHAPTER 1

Building Blocks

Atoms are incredibly small. There are more atoms in a speck of dust than there are grains of sand on a beach. Atoms of the same type are called **elements**. Chemists have found 92 different elements in nature. They have also created around 30 new elements in experiments. The elements are set out in a chart called the periodic table. This table groups together elements with similar properties.

Elements, such as sulfur, or metals like copper or zinc, are solids in nature. Their atoms line up in a repeating pattern called a **crystal structure**. If the atoms in a crystal could be seen under a powerful microscope, they would look like an organized stack of balls. Elements such as hydrogen and helium are gases in nature. In these elements, individual atoms or pairs of atoms float around in space.

Atoms are the building blocks of all matter. When the atoms of different elements come together, they can sometimes form chemical **bonds**. There are an enormous number of ways in which the atoms of different elements stick to each other to form molecules. These combinations produce the amazing variety of substances in the world.

Atoms of the elements sodium and chlorine combine to form crystals of common salt.

Looking at Atoms

Atoms are far too small to be seen with the naked eye. For example, an iron atom would have to be expanded to around ten million times its original size before it would be the same size as the head of a pin.

Scientists use microscopes to make very small objects look much bigger. The first microscopes were light microscopes, and they are still used today. Light passes

The angular crystals of tungsten metal can be seen clearly when viewed under a powerful electron microscope.

Fast Facts

- Fifty thousand atoms would fit in a row across the period at the end of this sentence.

- The world's first microscope was made in 1590 by two Dutch eyeglass makers.

- The first electron microscope was built in 1931 by scientists in Germany.

through a glass lens and into the eyes that are looking into the microscope. The light bends as it passes through the lens. This makes each side of the object being viewed appear farther apart. Good light microscopes magnify objects more than one thousand times before they become blurred. They are good for looking at tiny objects such as bacteria. But light microscopes are not powerful enough to see atoms.

Electron microscopes

Some modern microscopes use beams of tiny particles, called **electrons,** to look at very small objects. These electron microscopes magnify objects up to one million times their actual size. At this magnification, people can see some of the largest atoms. People look at the magnified object on a screen similar to a computer monitor.

Arranging atoms

Electron microscopes have shown that the atoms in many solids line up to form crystals. The atoms in a crystal are stacked together in regular, repeating patterns.

The way in which the atoms of elements are arranged often gives crystals a distinctive appearance. Diamonds consist of networks of carbon atoms. The carbon atoms are arranged in a regular pattern, which gives a diamond its beautiful appearance. Metals such as copper and silver are also made up of millions of atoms arranged in a regular crystal pattern.

An electron microscope uses a beam of electrons to scan objects too small to be seen with a light microscope.

Elements and Compounds

There are many different kinds of atoms. When a substance contains only one type of atom, it is known as an element. Scientists recognize more than 120 different elements, from hydrogen to uranium and beyond.

The properties of an element depend on the

Different atoms combine to form new substances. In this photograph, sodium atoms are combining with hydrogen and oxygen atoms in water to form molecules of sodium hydroxide.

 ? Did You Know?

Atoms can form a number of bonds with other atoms. In water, for example, one oxygen atom forms two bonds with two hydrogen atoms. The way in which the atoms bond gives the water molecule its shape.

type of atom from which it is made. Iron atoms group to form a strong, metallic crystal. Oxygen molecules form a light, colorless gas. Each oxygen molecule consists of two oxygen atoms. It is known as a diatomic molecule (*di* means "two").

Elements combine during chemical reactions. For example, iron reacts with oxygen to make iron oxide, or rust. Some reactions are violent—such as the reaction of sodium with water. When these two substances come into contact with each other they can explode in a huge fireball.

Many molecules

In many substances, the atoms are bonded as molecules. The atoms are tightly held within the molecules, but neighboring molecules may only stick to each other weakly. In liquids, such as water, the molecules are loosely held. They can slip past each other, so liquids can change their shape. In gases, such as oxygen, the molecules are so weakly attracted to each other that they drift apart.

This glass holds billions of water molecules. Each molecule is made up of two hydrogen atoms bonded to one oxygen atom.

Close up

Molecules come in many different shapes and sizes. The atoms that make up an oxygen molecule look like two balls stuck together. Water is more complex, with two hydrogen atoms stuck to one oxygen atom. More complex molecules can have rings or even spirals of atoms.

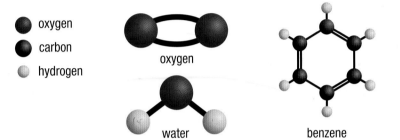

oxygen
carbon
hydrogen

oxygen

water

benzene

CHAPTER 2

Inside Atoms

Atoms are tiny, but they contain even smaller particles called electrons, **neutrons**, and **protons**. The neutrons and protons cluster together in the **nucleus** at the center of an atom. The electrons revolve around the nucleus in a way that is similar to how the planets orbit around the Sun.

Most of an atom is empty space. For example, if the nucleus of an atom could be expanded to the size of a golf ball, the electrons would be tiny points spinning 3 miles (5 kilometers) away from the center of the atom. Electrons weigh almost nothing compared to the protons and neutrons. As a result the nucleus contains most of the weight of the atom. The nucleus is held together by some of the strongest forces known to scientists.

Different elements have different numbers of protons in their nuclei. They also have different numbers of electrons revolving around their nuclei. For example, oxygen atoms always contain eight protons and eight electrons. The number of protons gives an atom its **atomic number**. Scientists use this number to label the different elements. For example, oxygen is labeled by its atomic number, 8.

When atoms collide with other atoms, the particles inside them can shoot out in all directions.

Electrifying Electrons

This photograph shows an electron's path (white spiral) inside a machine called a bubble chamber

The electrons of an atom revolve around the nucleus very quickly. They move around the nucleus in a series of energy levels called electron shells. A strong force, called the electromagnetic force, keeps the electrons revolving around the nucleus. This is the same force that produces the attraction between two magnets. The electromagnetic force can be incredibly strong.

The number of negatively charged electrons revolving around the nucleus of an atom is equal to the number of positively charged protons inside the nucleus. For example, there are always eight positively charged protons inside the nucleus of an oxygen atom. So there are always eight electrons revolving around the oxygen atom's nucleus to balance the charge. The positive charge of the nucleus is balanced by the negative charge

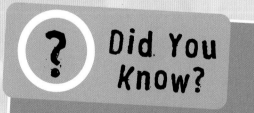

? Did You Know?

Metal atoms can share some of their electrons. The movement of the shared electrons through the metal is what we call electricity.

of the electrons, making the atom neutral overall. This powerful force of electrical attraction pulls the electrons and the protons together to make an atom.

Electrons and chemistry

Chemical reactions work because electrical forces, called chemical bonds, stick the atoms together like glue. An example is magnesium burning in air. Heat makes the magnesium react with oxygen in the air. An oxygen atom pulls two electrons from a magnesium atom to form a negative oxygen ion. The magnesium atom loses two electrons to form a positive magnesium ion. Opposite charges attract, and the two ions form a chemical bond. The compound produced is called magnesium oxide (MgO).

Fast Facts

- Most of an atom is made up of empty space.

- Each proton or neutron in the nucleus weighs almost 2,000 times more than an electron.

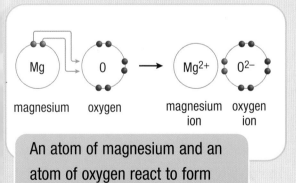

An atom of magnesium and an atom of oxygen react to form magnesium oxide.

When magnesium ribbon is heated in air, it glows with a brilliant white flame.

Looking Inside Atoms

Most scientists had no idea about what was inside an atom before the twentieth century. Some scientists thought that the nucleus was spread out like a ball, with the electrons trapped inside it. Other scientists had even stranger ideas. One respected physicist believed that atoms were hoops that would link together to make molecules.

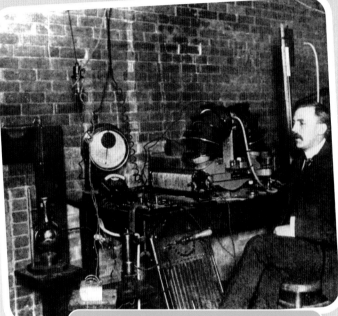

Ernest Rutherford is pictured at work in his laboratory at McGill University in Canada.

Rutherford's experiment

In 1909, Lord Ernest Rutherford (1871–1937) disproved these strange ideas. Rutherford designed an experiment in which tiny alpha particles were fired toward a thin film of gold foil. An alpha particle is made up of two protons and two neutrons. It is the same as the nucleus of a helium atom. In the experiment, most of the alpha particles shot straight through the foil. A few of them bounced back in the direction from which they came. Rutherford realized that these alpha particles were bouncing off tiny nuclei inside the atoms in the gold foil. Rutherford used math to figure out the size of the nucleus of a gold atom. He reasoned that it was about one-trillionth of a millimeter across.

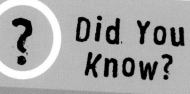

Did You Know?

New Zealand–born British physicist Ernest Rutherford had already won the 1908 Nobel Prize for Chemistry for his work on radioactivity before he figured out the structure of the atom.

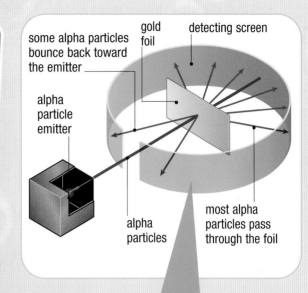

some alpha particles bounce back toward the emitter

gold foil

detecting screen

alpha particle emitter

alpha particles

most alpha particles pass through the foil

Close Up

In Rutherford's experiment, some alpha particles hit the gold nuclei and bounced back toward the source. Alpha particles are positively charged. Rutherford knew that the nucleus was also positively charged, because two positive charges push against each other. Rutherford also knew that the gold atoms were mostly empty space, because most of the alpha particles passed through the foil.

CHAPTER 3

Inside the Nucleus

The nuclei of most atoms contain two types of particles. One type has a positive electrical charge. It is called a proton. The second type weighs the same as a proton, but it does not carry an electrical charge. It is called a neutron.

Atoms of different elements have different numbers of protons and neutrons in their nuclei. Hydrogen is the simplest element. A hydrogen atom has one proton in its nucleus, but no neutrons. Uranium, with the atomic number 92, has 92 protons in its nucleus. The nucleus of a typical uranium atom has 146 neutrons. However, some uranium atoms have nuclei that contain 143 or 142 neutrons. These different types of atoms of the same element are called **isotopes**.

Two particles with like charges, such as protons, push against each other. So the force that binds protons in the nucleus must be very strong. For this reason it is called the **strong nuclear force**. Scientists have found a way to overcome the strong nuclear force. They can split apart atomic nuclei to unleash huge amounts of energy. This is what happens when an atomic bomb explodes. Nuclear reactors also split atomic nuclei to generate electricity.

An atomic bomb explodes in the Nevada desert. The bomb unleashes the huge amount of energy stored inside atomic nuclei.

Building Nuclei

Protons and neutrons are found inside the nuclei of every atom except for hydrogen. Hydrogen is unusual because it does not have any neutrons in its nucleus. It is made up of one proton and one electron. The positive proton balances the charge of the negative electron. The proton also adds to the atom's weight.

Neutrons in other atoms do not do very much apart from add to the atom's weight. The total number of protons and neutrons in an atom is called the **atomic weight**. With just a single proton, the atomic weight of hydrogen is 1. The nucleus of an oxygen atom usually contains eight protons and eight neutrons. So the atomic weight of oxygen is 16.

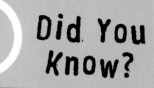

? Did You Know?

Protons and neutrons consist of even smaller particles called quarks. Each proton and neutron is a combination of three quarks, which are stuck together by a strong force.

This is a sample of uranium. This element has the heaviest naturally occurring nucleus. Most uranium atoms contain 235 protons and 146 neutrons in their nuclei.

Particle discovery

German scientist Wilhelm Wien (1864–1928) discovered protons in 1900. The discovery of the neutron came later in 1932. British scientist James Chadwick (1891–1974) accidentally made neutrons when he was looking at an element called boron.

Particle soup

Scientists have found many other mysterious particles besides protons, neutrons, and electrons. There are antiprotons, antineutrons, and positrons, which are the antiparticles of protons, neutrons, and electrons, respectively. If an antiparticle comes into contact with a normal particle, the two destroy each other. Some particles appear only at very high energies and quickly break down into normal particles. Scientists have peculiar names for these particles, such as "strange" and "charmed" particles.

The universe emerged following a big explosion called the Big Bang. The force of the explosion created fundamental particles such as quarks, which combined to make protons and neutrons.

? Did You Know?

Protons and neutrons formed a few seconds after the Big Bang created the universe. A few minutes after the Big Bang, the protons and neutrons combined to form atomic nuclei.

Isotopes and Radioactivity

Atoms of the same element are not always identical. There are different forms, called isotopes. An isotope has the same number of protons and electrons, but a different number of neutrons in its nucleus. Oxygen in air is a mixture of three isotopes. The atomic weight of these oxygen isotopes ranges from 16 to 18. Each isotope has eight protons in the nucleus, but one has eight neutrons, one has nine neutrons, and the third has ten neutrons.

Some isotopes are unstable. They break down into other isotopes or elements. Scientists call this process **radioactive decay**. One simple way in which nuclei can decay is when

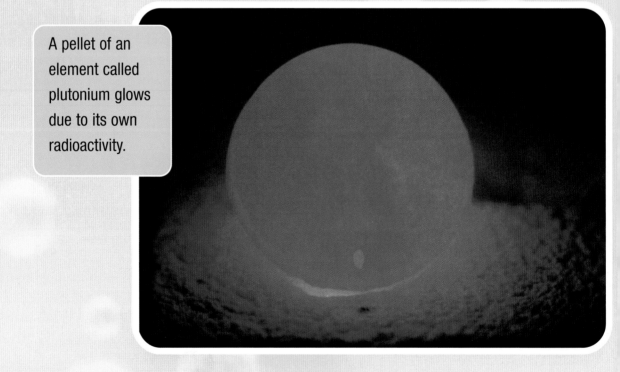

A pellet of an element called plutonium glows due to its own radioactivity.

they split apart and form two new nuclei. If these two nuclei are stable, they attract electrons and become new atoms.

Radioactivity

When an atom breaks down, the radioactivity can be both useful and very dangerous. **X-ray** machines are powered by radioactivity. They help doctors see inside the human body. But radioactive decay also powers the huge and damaging explosion of a nuclear bomb.

Fantastic forces

The strong nuclear force is the strongest known force in the

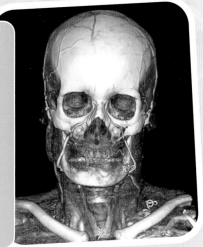

This picture of the head was made by combining X-ray images taken from around the body. X-ray machines are powered by radioactivity.

universe. Radioactive isotopes break down because the protons and neutrons can escape the strong force that holds them in the nucleus. This escape takes a long time. A uranium atom takes about a billion years to decay.

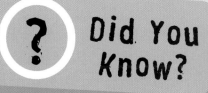

? Did You Know?

There are three hydrogen isotopes. The most common isotope has just one proton in the nucleus. Two rare hydrogen isotopes have nuclei with one and two neutrons combined with a single proton. They are called deuterium and tritium, respectively.

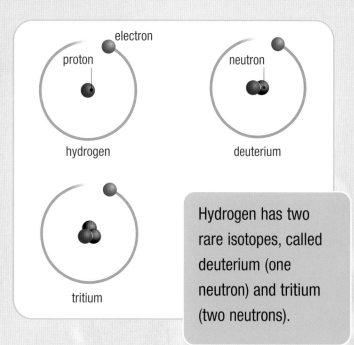

electron

proton

neutron

hydrogen

deuterium

tritium

Hydrogen has two rare isotopes, called deuterium (one neutron) and tritium (two neutrons).

Atom Smashers

In the 1930s, scientists were looking for cosmic rays—high-energy radiation from space. When the cosmic rays hit the atoms of metals such as lead, tiny particles sprayed out from the metal nuclei. The particles were much smaller than protons and neutrons. Scientists built **particle accelerators** to search for these particles. In a particle accelerator, atomic nuclei

These scientists are working at the Large Hadron Collider at CERN. They hope to find out more about dark matter by smashing protons together.

Fast Facts

The Large Hadron Collider at the European Organization for Nuclear Research (CERN) is the longest particle accelerator in the world. The tunnel for the accelerator is 17 miles (27 km) long and stretches across the border between France and Switzerland.

and other particles ride on waves of electromagnetic radiation. When the particles are moving at almost the speed of light, they are forced to collide. Scientists study the spray of particles resulting from the collision. The results have revealed some of the basic particles that make up matter and the forces that hold atoms together.

Different accelerators

There are two main types of particle accelerators. Both consist of a long track through which the particles accelerate up to the speed of light.

In a linear accelerator, particles move in a vacuum along a narrow copper tube. The particles ride on waves made by a machine called a klystron. Huge magnets keep the particles on a collision course with the target. Detectors reveal the results of the collision.

Circular accelerators do the same job as linear accelerators, but the particles move in a ring. Klystrons and magnets placed around the ring accelerate the particles to high speeds. Scientists then drop the target in front of the stream of particles.

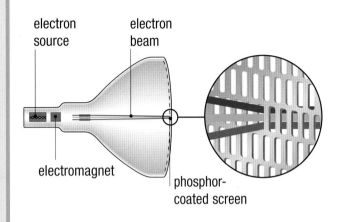

Close up

electron source

electron beam

electromagnet

phosphor-coated screen

The cathode-ray tube of an older-style TV or computer monitor is a particle accelerator. It uses electromagnets to accelerate electrons to very high speeds. When an electron smashes into a phosphor molecule in the screen, it glows as a tiny dot of light, called a pixel. A lot of pixels form an image on the screen.

Older-style television sets are simple particle accelerators. An image forms when a beam of electrons collide with the fluorescent screen.

CHAPTER 4

Living Atoms

Atoms bond as molecules of various shapes and sizes. Small molecules, such as the gases hydrogen and oxygen, contain two atoms held by a chemical bond. Networks of molecules can contain thousands, millions, or even billions of atoms bonded in complex ways. Molecular networks are vital for building the bodies of living things. The tiny **cells** inside the human body are factories for making and using these molecular networks.

Molecular networks are usually made up of carbon atoms. Carbon atoms can join end to end to make long chains and loops. When other atoms attach to the carbon chains, the molecule can often do useful tasks. For example, a molecule called hemoglobin in the blood carries oxygen around the body.

Using a technique called X-ray crystallography, scientists have figured out the shapes of many molecules. In 1953, two scientists famously used the technique to figure out the shape of a molecule of deoxyribonucleic acid (**DNA**). Because of X-ray crystallography, scientists now know the shapes of many protein molecules. They have even seen the shapes of viruses such as those that cause the common cold.

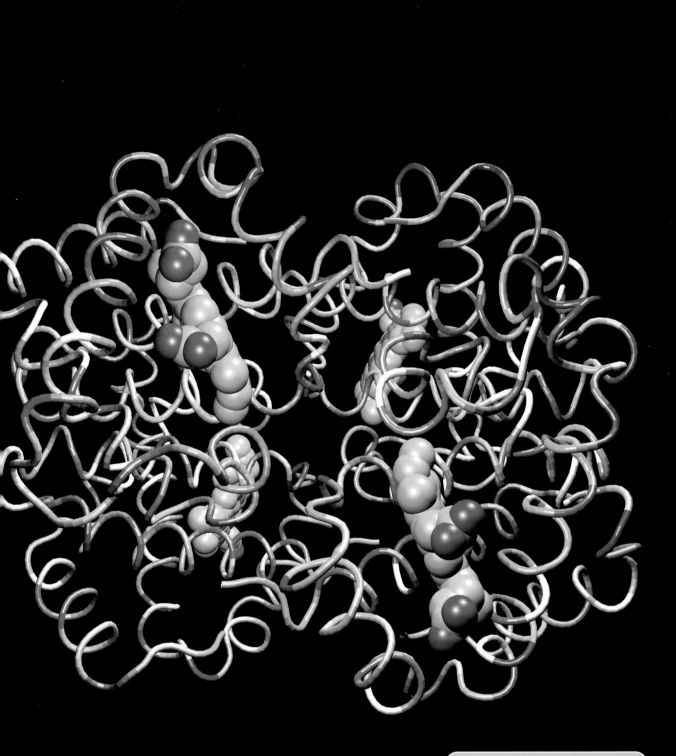

Long chains of carbon atoms join up to form a molecule of hemoglobin, shown here as a computer-generated model.

Molecules of Life

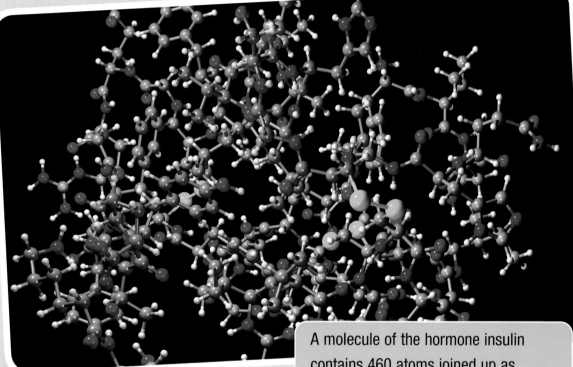

A molecule of the hormone insulin contains 460 atoms joined up as 51 amino acids. Insulin controls the amount of sugar in the bloodstream.

The human body needs three main molecules to work properly. Fats and carbohydrates give the body the energy it needs. Proteins help to build up body tissues and muscles.

Carbohydrates and fats are made up of long chains of carbon atoms joined end to end. For example, a carbohydrate called starch may include more than ten thousand carbon chains joined in a long line.

Proteins are much more complex than carbohydrates or fats. Proteins are made up of smaller subunits called amino acids. There are twenty basic amino acids. Hundreds or thousands of these different amino acids combine to make molecules with complex shapes. Some of these

develop diseases such as some forms of cancer. The information is written as a code in the DNA molecule. Almost every cell in the human body has DNA. The only cells that do not contain DNA are red blood cells.

proteins build tissues and regulate the chemical reactions that keep the body alive. Other protein molecules, called hormones, send messages through the bloodstream. For example, the hormone insulin helps the body to regulate the amount of sugar in the blood.

DNA molecules

Deoxyribonucleic acid (DNA) is the blueprint for life. It contains all the instructions for building the different parts of the human body. The instructions result in different physical characteristics, such as eye and hair color. The instructions also tell people if they are likely to

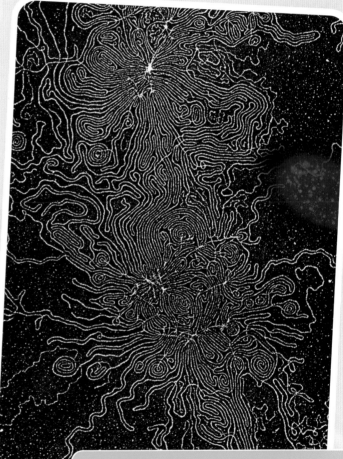

An electron microscope reveals the tiny strand of DNA inside a human cell. Stretched out, the DNA strand would be several miles in length.

Unraveling DNA

One of the most amazing scientific discoveries of the twentieth century was figuring out the structure of the DNA molecule. In 1953, American scientist James Watson (born 1928) and British biologist Francis Crick (1916–2004) showed that DNA is in a long, twisted structure called a double helix.

You can picture this double helix shape by thinking of DNA as a long ladder. Now imagine the ladder is twisted so that its two sides are wrapped around each other. Each side of the ladder makes a spiral shape called a helix, similar to the thread of a screw. Since both sides of the ladder have helix shapes, the overall shape is a "double helix."

This computer model of DNA was formed using the results from experiments in X-ray crystallography.

Close up

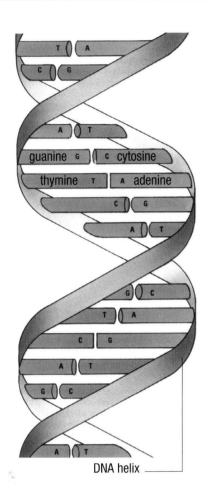

DNA helix

There are four different chemicals that make up the steps of the DNA ladder. They are adenine (A), cytosine (C), guanine (G), and thymine (T). A and T pair up to form one step of the ladder. C and G pair up to form another step. The instructions for life are written in these steps.

Watson (left), Crick (right), and Franklin (below) figured out the structure for DNA in 1953.

X-ray vision

Crick and Watson figured out the shape of DNA using photographs taken by British scientist Rosalind Franklin (1920–1958). Franklin used X rays to look at the shapes of DNA molecules. An X ray is similar to visible light, but it carries some more energy.

People use X rays to study the shape of DNA. First, scientists grow crystals of DNA. Then they shine X rays through the crystal. This reveals a pattern of bright and dark spots, similar to the sparkling effect as light shines through a diamond. Scientists use complex math to figure out the shape of the DNA molecule from the pattern of spots.

CHAPTER 5

Computer Chips

Understanding how atoms work is key to understanding the complex world of modern computer chips. Modern chips are about the same size as a postage stamp. Each one contains billions of tiny electronic switches called **transistors**. Computers work by switching the transistors on and off to compute the answers to calculations. More transistors means faster calculations.

When the first computers appeared in the 1940s, transistors had not been invented. The switches of these early computers were made from vacuum tubes. These devices were very big, and an early computer filled an entire room.

Each transistor in a modern computer chip is only about one hundred atoms wide. Every year, newer, smaller chips include more transistors to make faster, more efficient computers.

As technology advances, modern computers become faster and faster, and the parts from which they are made shrink in size. Just as the computers of today are millions of times faster than those of sixty years ago, it is expected that future technology will be much more powerful than that of today.

Modern computer chips are tiny devices. An electron microscope is needed to see the tiny tracks that form the electrical circuits.

Clever Chips

Microchips are everywhere—in the television, DVD recorder, microwave oven, personal computer, dishwasher, and family car. These tiny chips act like brains to control the devices. The chips inside DVD recorders might remember to record a television show and turn the recorder off at the correct time.

The microchip in the middle of this picture is the "brain," or control center, of a computer. It processes billions of calculations every second.

Math machines

Computer chips do two main tasks. They perform calculations and they store the answers. The calculating chip inside a modern computer is called a central processing unit, or CPU. The storage chip is called the memory. Computers do everything in numbers. One sequence of numbers could say which mouse button controls something, while another could say which key activates the printer. The CPU uses the number codes to decide what to do next. The memory stores these codes for later use.

Bits and bytes

A memory chip remembers all the number codes by recording the position of all the transistors. Each transistor stores one binary digit, or **bit**. If the transistor is off, the chip stores a zero. If the transistor is on, the chip stores a one. The computer combines all the different zeros and ones to represent different numbers. Eight bits combine to make one **byte**, which can represent any number from 0 to 255. Modern memory chips can store billions of bytes. This is as much information as you could fit into thousands of books.

Processing power

Computer scientists describe a CPU by how many instructions it can do in one second. Computer speed is measured in units called gigahertz. A CPU speed of two gigahertz can process up to two billion calculations per second. This processing power allows computers to carry out amazing calculations—for example, making computer games look as realistic as movies.

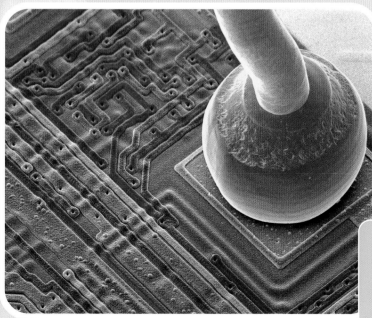

The wires that connect the different parts of a microchip together can only be seen under an electron microscope.

Making Chips

Microchips are made from silicon. This hard, gray element is special because it is a **semiconductor**. This means that silicon can behave both as a metal and a nonmetal. In some cases, electricity can flow through silicon like a metal. In other cases, it resists electricity like a nonmetal.

Scientists grow perfect crystals of pure silicon to make computer chips. These crystals are cut into

Fast Facts

- By 2008, the world computer industry had built two billion personal computers.

- Billions of transistors could fit on a chip about the same size as a postage stamp.

thin wafers with about the same thickness as a fingernail. The wafer is then coated with a chemical called a resist. An outline of the circuit is put on the wafer and a beam of laser light is shone onto the wafer. The laser light hardens the resist. The unhardened resist is dissolved, and the silicon is

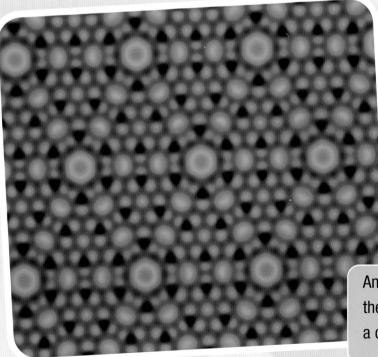

An electron microscope reveals the repeating pattern of atoms in a crystal of pure silicon.

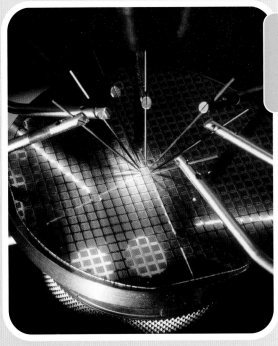

Rows of microchips are made on a single wafer of silicon. Probes test each chip to ensure that the circuits are working properly.

Moore's law is important because more transistors mean better chips. Computer speed becomes faster, memory storage is larger, and devices are smaller. This progress has affected many new technologies, from cellphones to MP3 players and digital cameras. In the future, new inventions that use microtechnology will continue to change our lives in new and exciting ways.

exposed to chemicals to carve a circuit onto the chip.

Advancing technology

For more than fifty years, computer technology follows a trend known as Moore's law. Named after computer scientist Gordon Moore (born 1929), the law states that the number of transistors on a computer chip will double every two years. In the early 1970s, there were thousands of transistors on a single chip. By the 1980s this number became millions. Now there are billions of transistors on the most advanced chips.

A technician puts a silicon wafer into an oven. Heat hardens the chemicals that form the chip's circuitry.

CHAPTER 6

Miniature Technology

As technology advances, new devices are becoming smaller and smaller. Modern science has reached the point where some devices are being made that are just a few hundred atoms wide. This miniaturization of technology is called nanotechnology.

The idea of nanotechnology came in 1959, when American scientist Richard Feynman (1918–1988) gave a speech to the American Physical Society. In his speech, Feynman highlighted the scope for science on a microscopic level. At the end of his speech Feynman issued two challenges. He offered $10,000 to the first person who could make a working electric **motor** just a fraction of an inch wide. Feynman offered another $10,000 to the first person who could reduce the size of their writing by 25,000 times. It took another 25 years for these prizes to be claimed.

Nanotechnology offers some amazing applications. For example, scientists are developing miniature machines that can repair damage to the human body from the inside. Scientists are also developing strong materials that are used to make many products, such as electrical wires and cables for skyscrapers.

The blue line running down the center of this picture is an electrical wire that measures just 10 carbon atoms wide. It may be used to power miniature machines of the future.

Nanotechnology

The tiny purple squares on this computer chip are pressure sensors. The sensors set off a car's air bag in the event of an emergency. The tip of a pencil shows how small these sensors are.

Imagine a tiny wheel that measures just ten **nanometers** across. One hundred million of these miniature wheels would fit across a yardstick. If each wheel could expand to the size of a coin, the wheels would cover 650,000 miles (1,000,000 km). That is three times the distance between Earth and the Moon.

The words *micro* and *nano* are used to describe very small objects—microorganisms, microprocessors, nanostructures, and even the iPod "Nano." However, scientists use these words in a precise way. The word *micro* means "one-millionth" and *nano* means "one-billionth." (There are one million **micrometers** and one billion nanometers in a meter.) So nanotechnology looks at devices that are billionths of a meter in size.

Nanotechnology today

Most people have embraced the use of nanotechnology without really realizing it. Over the last few years, many household items have begun to include nano-sized materials. For example, many products use fine powders in which each grain measures just tens of atoms across. Sunscreens use nano-sized powders that are so small they do not leave white marks on the skin as larger-sized powders would.

Modern computer chips have also embraced the use of nanotechnology devices. The individual components of electronic computers are now just tens of nanometers across, or about one hundred atoms wide. Other devices with nano-sized parts are becoming increasingly available. They include the tiny sensors used to detect chemicals in the air and flexible digital-screen technology.

Fast Facts

● One nanometer is one hundred thousand times smaller than the width of a human hair.

● The prefix *nano* comes from a Greek word meaning "dwarf."

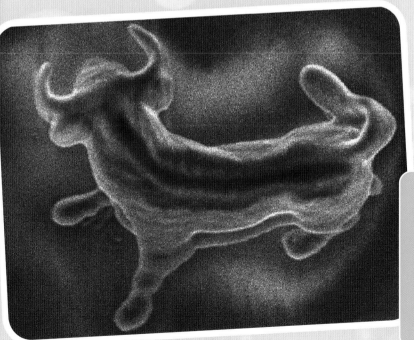

Modern art has also embraced nanotechnology. This image of a bull has been carved on a silicon wafer. It measures 6 microns across, which is about the same size as a tiny red blood cell.

Nanotubes and Nanoballs

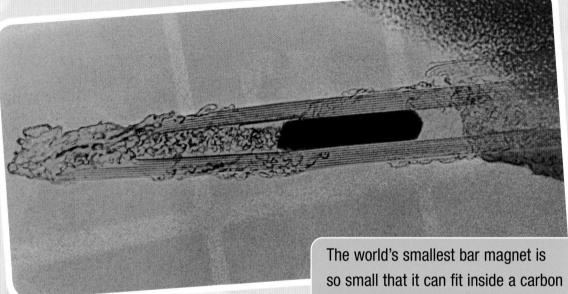

The world's smallest bar magnet is so small that it can fit inside a carbon nanotube. The center of the tube is just 15 nanometers across.

Most people are familiar with two very different forms of carbon—the graphite in a pencil lead and the diamonds in engagement rings and other jewelry. Each carbon atom in graphite links up to three other carbon atoms in loosely held sheets. This makes the graphite soft and able to mark paper. In diamond, the carbon atoms connect to four other atoms. The carbon atoms are locked in a rigid network, which makes diamond one of the strongest and hardest substances in the world.

Tiny tubes

Scientists have built other forms of carbon for use in nanotechnology. They are particularly excited about tiny tubular structures of carbon atoms. Called carbon nanotubes, these structures form as sheets of carbon atoms roll up like a piece of paper rolls up into a tube. These carbon nanotubes have the same strength as diamond, but they are made as long, flexible wires. They are good conductors of electricity, which makes them ideal for electronics. The downside is that they are very expensive. Carbon nanotubes are more expensive by weight than diamonds or gold.

Nanoballs

Carbon atoms can also join together to form hollow spheres known as nanoballs. Carbon nanoballs were first discovered in 1985 by a team of physicists working at the University of Sussex in Britain. Nanoballs have some far-reaching applications. For example, scientists are looking at using nanoballs to deliver drugs directly to the target tissues inside the human body.

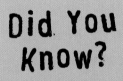

? Did You Know?

Carbon nanomaterials are strong, so they could allow people to build enormous skyscrapers several miles high. One amazing idea is to use cables made from carbon nanotubes for a space elevator that can carry people and goods into orbit.

An artist's impression shows what the space elevator might look like.

Nanomachines

As nanotechnology becomes more popular, scientists are looking to make tiny machines on the scale of nanometers. They have already built motors that are just a few hundred nanometers across. They have also made tiny nano-sized wheels and springs. These miniature machines have no uses at the moment. In the future, however, scientists may be able to connect them to make useful mechanical devices that are just a few hundred atoms across.

The possibilities for nanomachines have not yet been fully explored. Some people think that millions of nanorobots could build and repair tiny objects. Future nanomachines could even help to cure illness and disease. Tiny nano-sized devices could circulate in the bloodstream, attacking the germs that cause illness. These medical nanomachines might also repair the body, allowing people to live longer and lead more healthy lives.

These tiny gears could be used to power a system of microsensors. These sensors could detect the properties of certain chemicals.

Conclusion

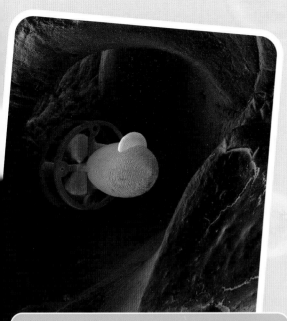

This is an artist's impression of a tiny submarine. In the future, it might be able to detect and repair defects inside small parts of the human body.

During the twentieth century, scientists made many important discoveries about atoms. Their experiments revealed that atoms are made up of tiny particles held together by incredibly strong forces. They realized that atoms are the building blocks of all matter and bond together to form molecules that make up larger substances.

Scientists are still learning about atoms. They use particle accelerators to smash atoms together at high speed. Through these experiments with atoms, scientists hope to find out more about the forces that hold the universe together. Their research is also leading to new technologies. These include powerful computer chips that can fit on your fingernail and machines that are just a few hundred atoms wide.

No one can predict the future. But the scientists of the twenty-first century will continue to investigate the challenges of the invisible world of atoms and molecules.

Looking to the future

It is hard to figure out exactly how nanotechnology will change our lives and the world in which we live. Imagine what life must have been like two hundred years ago, before airplanes, personal computers, lasers, rockets, telephones, and televisions were invented. Two hundred years from now, the world will have changed in even more incredible ways because of new developments in nanotechnology.

Glossary

atomic number The atomic number is the number of protons in the nucleus of an atom.

atomic weight The atomic weight is the number of protons and neutrons in an atomic nucleus.

bit A single unit of information with two values—0 (off) and 1 (on)—is called a bit.

bonds Chemical bonds are the forces that hold atoms together.

byte A byte is a unit of information formed from eight bits.

cells The smallest units of the human body are called cells.

crystal structure The regular pattern of atoms in a solid is called the crystal structure.

DNA Short for deoxyribonucleic acid, DNA molecules contain the instructions for life.

electrons Negatively charged particles called electrons revolve around the nucleus of an atom.

elements Fundamental substances called elements contain only one type of atom.

isotopes These types of atoms have the same number of protons but different numbers of neutrons.

micrometer One micrometer is one millionth of a meter.

molecules A molecule is made up of two or more atoms held together by chemical bonds.

motor A motor is a machine or engine that causes movement.

nanometer One nanometer is one billionth of a meter.

neutrons Electrically uncharged particles called neutrons are found in the nucleus of an atom.

nucleus The nucleus is the dense core at the center of an atom.

particle accelerators Machines called particle accelerators are used to smash particles such as atoms together.

protons Positively charged particles called protons are found in the nucleus of an atom.

radioactive decay This process is when an atomic nucleus breaks down.

semiconductor A semiconductor can either stop or allow electricity to flow through it.

strong nuclear force The powerful strong nuclear force holds neutrons and protons inside the nucleus.

transistors These electronic devices work as switches.

X ray An X ray is an energetic form of light.

Find Out More

Books

Claybourne, Anna. *Microworlds: Unlocking the Secrets of Atoms and Molecules: Physical Science*. Vero Beach, Florida: Rourke Publishing, 2007.

Johnson, Rebecca L. *Nanotechnology*. Minneapolis, Minnesota: Lerner Publications, 2005.

Saunders, Nigel. *Atoms and Molecules (The Physical Sciences)*. London, England: Wayland, 2007.

Spilsbury, Louise, and Richard Spilsbury. *Building Blocks of Matter: Atoms and Molecules*. Portsmouth, New Hampshire: Heinemann Library, 2008.

Stille, Darlene R. *Atoms & Molecules: Building Blocks of the Universe*. Mankato, Minnesota: Compass Point Books, 2007.

Websites

http://www.howstuffworks.com/atom-smasher.htm
The award-winning How Stuff Works website explains how particle accelerators work and how they have helped scientists learn more about the particles inside atoms.

http://www.ksnn.larc.nasa.gov/webtext.cfm?unit=nanotech
NASA's Kids Science News Network website includes animations, videos, and a quiz to help you explore the world of nanotechnology.

http://www.lbl.gov/abc/Basic.html
This website explains the structure of atoms as well as isotopes and radioactivity, cosmic rays, and nuclear fusion. The site includes a helpful glossary of unusual terms.

Index

Page numbers in **boldface** are illustrations.